LIVING OUT OF THE MOMENT

"IF YOU CANNOT LAUGH AT YOURSELF, I WILL LAUGH AT YOU."
THE COSMIC GIGGLE

The Publisher totally denies having ever read
this manuscript. It therefore cannot, nor would it in any case,
take reponsibility for the contents of this book . . .
whatever it might be.
THE PUBLISHER

LIVING OUT OF THE MOMENT

100 WAYS TO OBTAIN HAPPINESS THROUGH TOTAL DENIAL

A DESCENDENTAL HUMOR BOOK

BY GURU BABALOO RUM DUST

First published in 1995 by Charles E. Tuttle Co., Inc.
of Rutland, Vermont and Tokyo, Japan, with editorial offices at
153 Milk Street Boston, Massachusetts 02109

©1995 Ron Schultz

All rights reserved. No part of this publication may be reproduced or utilized in any form whatsoever without prior written permission from the publisher.
ISBN 0-8048-3073-8

Design by Learning Arts Publications

Illustrations by Esther Szegedy

1 3 5 7 9 10 8 6 4 2   02 01 00 99 98 97 96 95

Printed in the United States of America

INTRODUCTION

As, I'm sure, many of you are already well aware, I am the father of Descendentalism. For those of you who have yet to be exposed to our vision of the way of this world, Descendentalism is based on that ancient and time-honored concept, The Principle of Avoidance, which, for what may appear to be rather obvious reasons, has never been recorded until this writing. The Descendental path was founded on the bedrock of the practice of Total Denial.

Perhaps, your first introduction to Descendental thought came through our many classes in Descendental Meditation. Unlike other forms of mind quieting, DM, as we prefer, offers total distraction, allowing the meditant to find a place of complete avoidance and ultimate happiness. Total Denial, or TD as many initiates refer to it, is but a vehicle to maintain this space of abundant escape.

Once an initiate has joined the Descendental movement, there are literally minutes of practice necessary before mastery occurs. You may see around you, in every aspect of your life, many of our most ardent followers practicing total denial in perfect avoidance. You may live with them or work with them. The popularity of our movement has brought them everywhere. We must honor these masters as we honor all great spiritual beings. Or we can ignore them thoroughly, and thereby become one with their path.

What will follow are but a fraction of the ways to obtain happiness through Total Denial. But after only fleeting consideration of these 100 aphorisms of evasion the boundlessness of Descendentalism should be totally clear to you, and you can join the glorious multitudes effectively practicing avoidance in the world today.

Without commitment,
I am certainly,

GURU BABALOO RUM DUST

LIVING OUT OF THE MOMENT

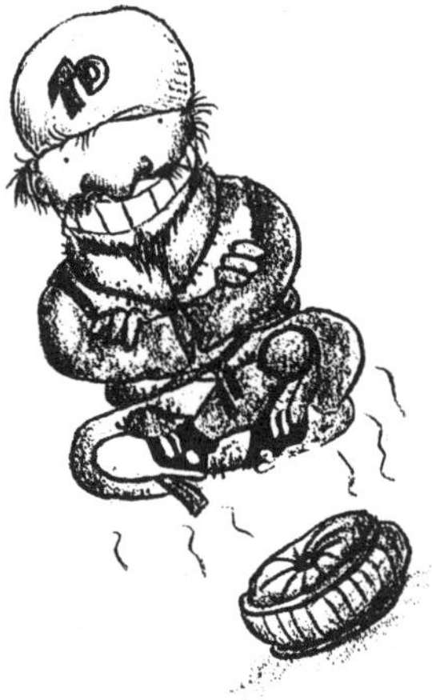

1. IGNORE ALL FEEDBACK
   FOCUS NOT ON THE SOUND, BUT ONLY ON THE MOVEMENT OF YOUR ACCUSER'S LIPS.

2. **BETRAY ALL PERSONAL CONFIDENCES**
   A SECRET KEPT IS AN OPPORTUNITY LOST.

3. **SANCTION IMPROPRIETY IN PUBLIC PLACES**
   IT IS NOT THE MANNERS OF RIGHTEOUSNESS THAT FURTHER HAPPINESS, BUT THE ABILITY TO PASS GAS AT WILL.

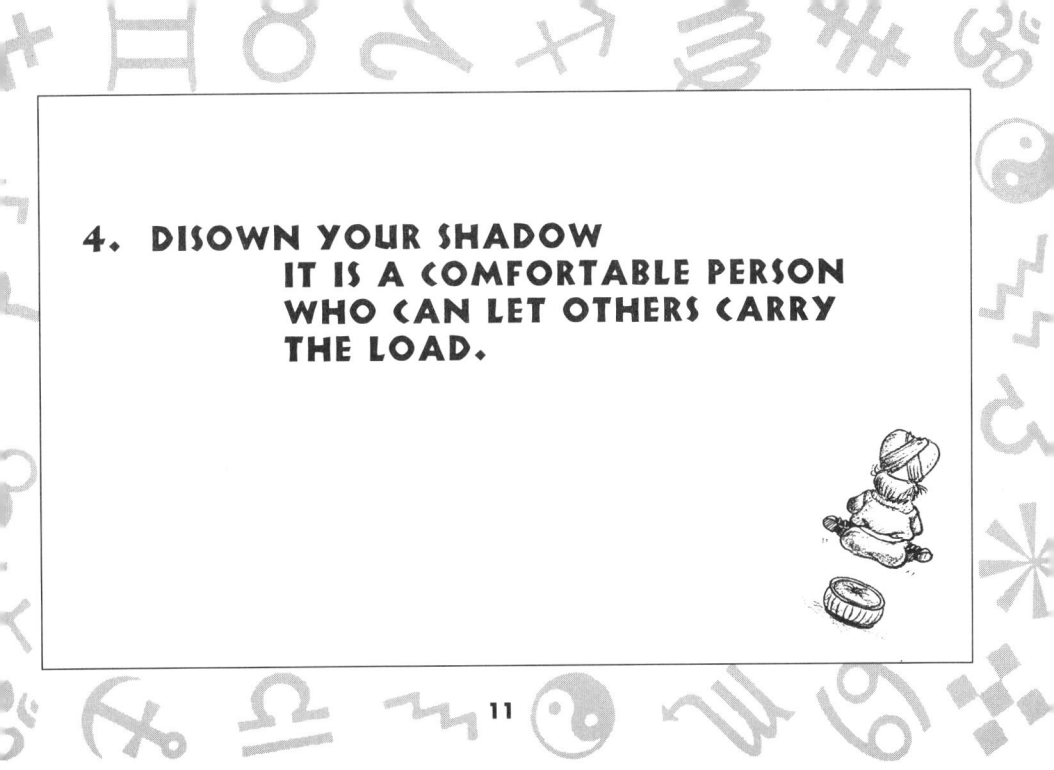

4. DISOWN YOUR SHADOW
   IT IS A COMFORTABLE PERSON
   WHO CAN LET OTHERS CARRY
   THE LOAD.

5. CULTIVATE AN INNER SHALLOWNESS IN ALL YOU DO

      DO NOT BE FOOLED BY THE DEPTH OF YOUR OWN SUPERFICIALITY.

**6. ABANDON ANY QUEST FOR TRUTH
FICTION IS SCARY ENOUGH.**

**7. CEDE INTELLECTUAL INVOLVEMENT
FOLLOW YOUR IGNORANCE.**

8. **SURRENDER OBJECTIVITY WHEN DEALING WITH INFERIORS**
   SUBMIT TO PREJUDICE AND DISLIKE EVERYONE EQUALLY.

9. **ALWAYS ASSUME WHAT OTHERS THINK OR FEEL**
   WHO KNOWS BETTER WHAT YOU REALLY WANT FROM OTHERS?

10. SOW DISCORD IN GROUP ENCOUNTERS HARMONY CAN ONLY LEAD TO COMMUNITY SINGS.

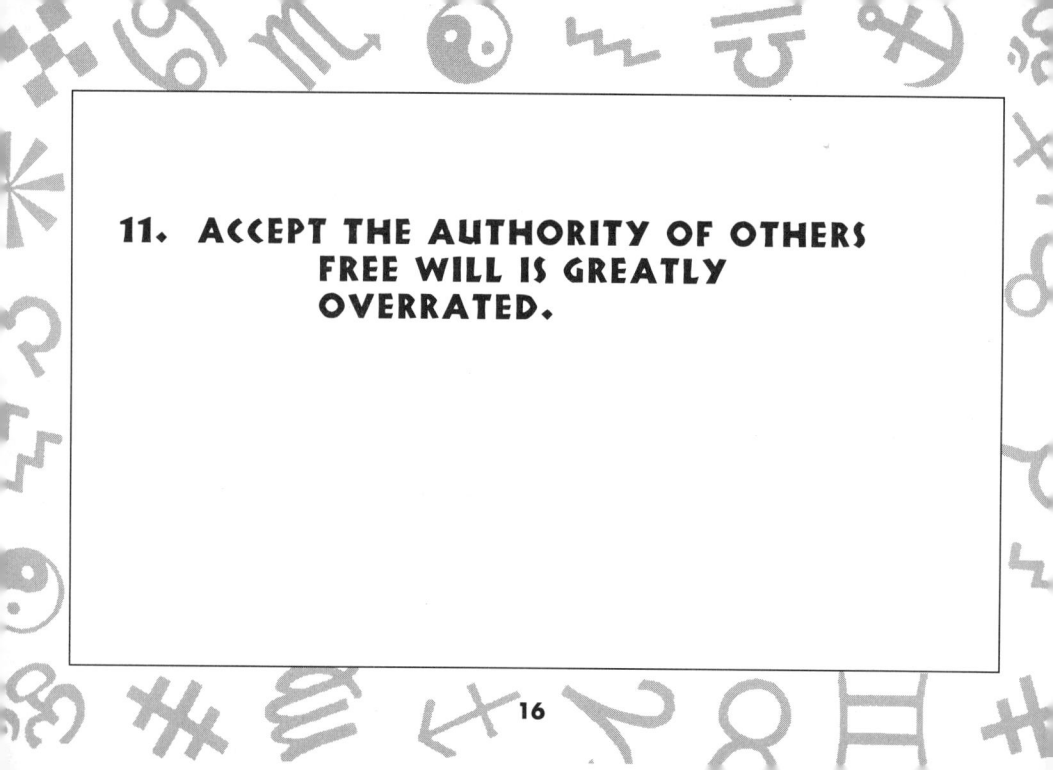

11. ACCEPT THE AUTHORITY OF OTHERS FREE WILL IS GREATLY OVERRATED.

12. **MATERIALIZE WELFARE PROSPERITY ONLY ALWAYS REMEMBER TO CALL IT A SPACE STATION.**

13. **DISREGARD ALL TELEPATHIC COMMUNICATIONS ESPECIALLY WHEN THEY CALL COLLECT.**

14. SHUN EXERCISES IN HIGHER CONSCIOUSNESS
   ATTEMPT NOT TO UNDERSTAND THE WORKINGS OF THE INNER MIND, IT CAN ONLY LEAD TO RIDE SHARING.

15. DOUBT NOTHING
   IT REQUIRES FAR TOO MUCH THOUGHT.

**16. ENCOURAGE PROJECTION
PROJECT ONTO OTHERS WHAT
YOU WOULD NOT HAVE
PROJECTED ONTO YOURSELF.**

17. DEFEND ANAL COMPULSION
    KEEPING THINGS IN THEIR PLACE
    IS THE ONLY PLACE TO BE.

18. NEUTRALIZE CLAIRVOYANCE
    OR IS THAT A BRIDGE I SEE IN
    YOUR FUTURE?

19. RESOLVE YOURSELF TO RESIGNATION EMBRACE THE QUITTER, THE FIRST TO DRINK COLD BEER.

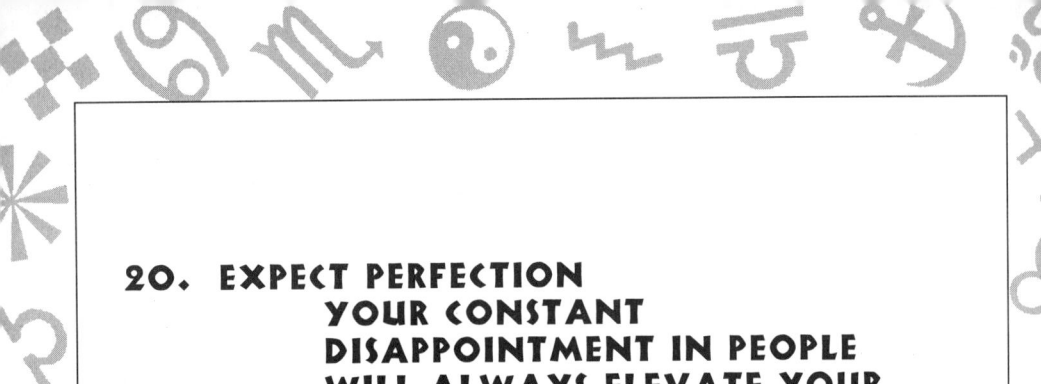

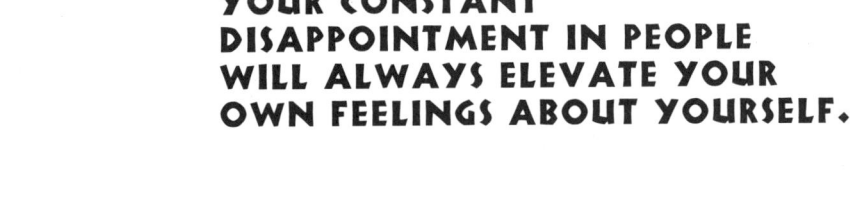

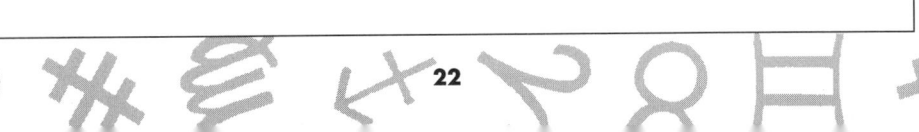

20. EXPECT PERFECTION YOUR CONSTANT DISAPPOINTMENT IN PEOPLE WILL ALWAYS ELEVATE YOUR OWN FEELINGS ABOUT YOURSELF.

21. **DISAVOW DETERMINATION
       PERSEVERANCE FRUSTRATES.**

22. **POSTPONE COMMITMENT
       WHY BE BOUND BY THE
       NEEDS OF OTHERS?**

23. ESCAPE AT ANY COST
   IF YOU ARE NOT WHERE YOU ARE, YOU CAN NEVER BE FOUND.

24. FEIGN ILLNESS WHEN ASKED FOR AN OPINION
   BETTER A LITTLE CHICKEN SOUP THAN UPSETTING YOUR MOTHER.

25. PRACTICE INTOLERANCE WITHOUT ATTACHMENT
    WHEN THE LIGHT CHANGES,
    THE HORN HONKS.
    NO EYE CONTACT.

26. REFRAIN FROM ALL CONTEMPLATION
   A ROLLING MIND GATHERS
   NO MOSS.

27. SUCCUMB TO TEMPTATION
   AS THE WISE HEDON OF
   HAMLIN HAS SAID,
   "AS LONG AS YOU KNOW BETTER,
   IT'S ALL RIGHT."

28. CASTIGATE THE VIRTUOUS DEBAUCHERY IS ITS OWN REWARD.

29. SCORN ALL OPPORTUNITY
   THE RAT RACE IS WON ONLY
   BY RATS.

30. QUESTION CERTAINTY
   THE RIGHTER YOU ARE,
   THE WRONGER YOU'LL BE.

**31. RESIST REFLECTION
SHALLOWNESS HARBORS
NO BILGE.**

32. PERPETUATE CONCEIT
    NARCISSISM IS
    LOVE ETERNAL.

33. MISLEAD YOURSELF AND OTHERS
   INVEST IN YOUR DELUSIONS OF GRANDEUR.

34. FABRICATE CONTEMPT FOR NEW ACQUAINTANCES
   STRIKE FIRST AND AVOID THE NEED TO PROVE YOURSELF WISER.

35. EXACT REVENGE
   AN OPPORTUNITY TO RETALIATE
   IS THE UNIVERSE PROVIDING
   A SIMPLE PLEASURE.

36. PROMOTE IMBALANCE
   A LOOSE CANNON HAS FEW
   ADVERSARIES.

37. DELAY PATIENCE
   HOW MUCH EASIER IS IT TO
   FLY OFF THE HANDLE THAN
   TO WAIT FOR INFORMATION
   YOU DO NOT WANT.

38. **MANIFEST DYSFUNCTION**
    TOO MUCH LOVE CAN ACTUALLY BRING FAMILY MEMBERS TOGETHER—A TERRIFYING THOUGHT.

39. **STIMULATE SIN IN THOSE YOU MEET**
    FOLLOWING THE PATH OF CONSTANT GRATIFICATION CAN ONLY TAKE YOU TO A LAND OF SUPREME SATISFACTION.

40. AVOID LISTENING TO UNDERLINGS REAL COMMUNICATION WILL ONLY ENCOURAGE THEM TO TALK MORE.

41. FOSTER INDISCRETION WITHOUT PROVOCATION
   DO NOT CONCERN YOURSELF WITH THE ANGER OF THE CUCKOLD, WHEN THE PLEASURES OF THE FLESH AVAIL THEMSELVES.

42. PROMOTE SELF-INDULGENCE
   EXTREMISM WHEN SHOPPING IS NO VICE.

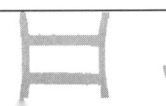

43. ADVOCATE BAD TASTE
   ART IS NOTHING BUT THE
   DECEPTION OF THOSE WITH
   TOO MUCH TIME ON
   THEIR HANDS.

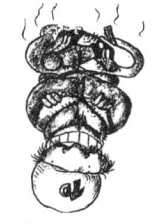

44. SHAME WITHOUT BLAME
YOU CAN ONLY MAKE PEOPLE FEEL AS BAD AS THEY WANT TO FEEL.

**45. RUN AWAY FROM CONFRONTATION
SWIFT LEGS ALWAYS LEAVE
COURAGE IN THE DUST.**

**46. DODGE REALITY
NEVER ASSUME THAT THINGS
ARE REALLY HOW THEY ARE.**

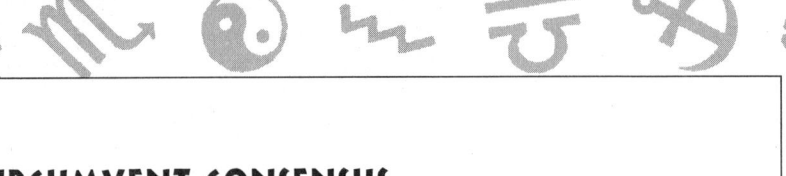

47. CIRCUMVENT CONSENSUS
   TO BE OBTUSE IS TO NEVER HAVE TO SAY YOU'VE DECIDED.

48. OPPOSE CONVICTIONS WHEN CONSIDERING A LIFE PATH
   NEVER TAKE A STAND THAT COULD BE MISCONSTRUED AS A COMMITMENT.

49. DISREGARD ANY LATE NOTICES
   IT IS BETTER TO SIT IN THE DARK
   THAN TO BECOME ENTANGLED IN
   A WEB OF CORPORATE CORRUPTION.

50. SIDESTEP ALL AGREEMENTS
   THE WISE PERSON KNOWS A
   LAWSUIT CANNOT FOLLOW WHERE
   PEN HAS NOT MET PAPER.

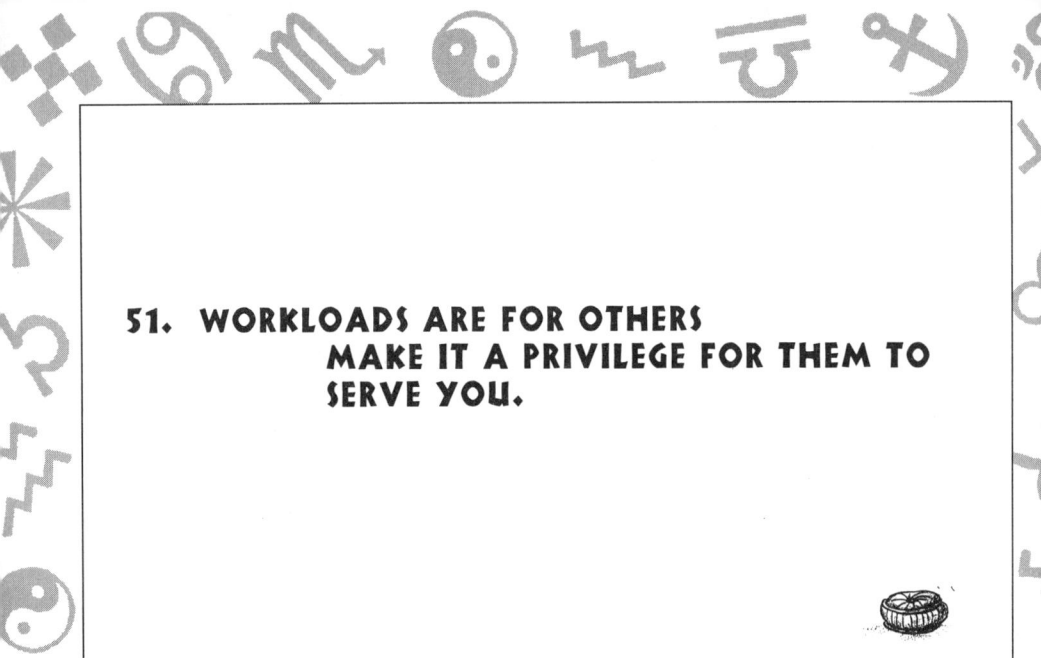

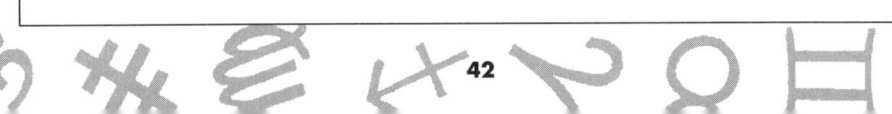

**51. WORKLOADS ARE FOR OTHERS
      MAKE IT A PRIVILEGE FOR THEM TO
      SERVE YOU.**

52. ESCHEW RECONCILIATION
   DOES A BLACK WIDOW SPIDER EVER APOLOGIZE TO HER MATE?

53. SPURN FORTITUDE
   THE EFFORT IS NEVER WORTH THE MOUNTAIN MOVED.

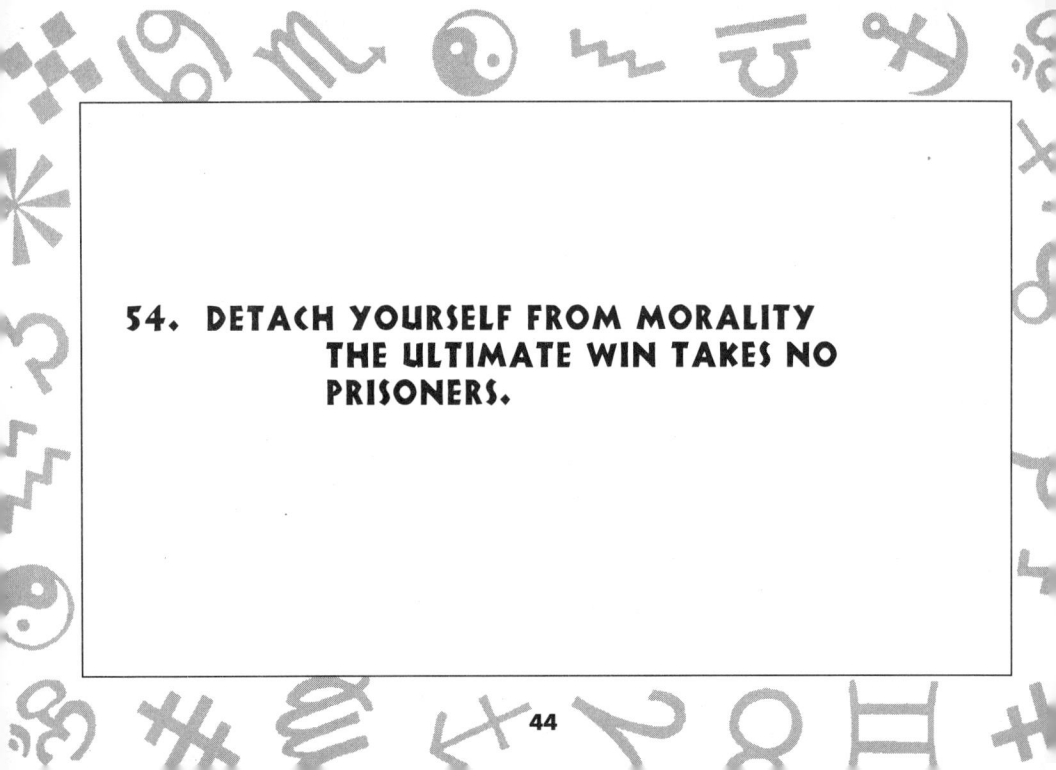

**54. DETACH YOURSELF FROM MORALITY
THE ULTIMATE WIN TAKES NO PRISONERS.**

55. DISDAIN EVERY CHANGE REQUEST
   ALL ROADS LEAD TO ENTROPY.

56. FORSAKE ALL FAITH
   ACCORDING TO THE USED CAR BLUE BOOK, IT IS BETTER TO BUY NOTHING THAN TO PURCHASE SOMETHING YOU CANNOT TOUCH.

57. ACCEPT NO ACCOUNTABILITY FOR DEADLINES
    MEMORY IS THE SECOND THING TO GO.

58. PACIFY THROUGH INDIFFERENCE
    COMPLACENCY BEGETS A PEACEFUL STUPOR.

**59. SCHEDULE ONLY GRATIFICATION
LIFE IS SIMPLY TOO SHORT FOR
ANYTHING LESS.**

60. CENSURE MODESTY
         IF YOU'VE GOT IT, FLAUNT IT.

**61. ACTIVELY DELAY MEETING OBJECTIVES
GOALS ARE MERELY THE
OUTCOME OF ANXIOUS MINDS.**

**62. HONOR POMPOSITY
PREPONDERANCE IN WORD AND
DEED IS SELF-FULFILLING
PROGNOSTICATION.**

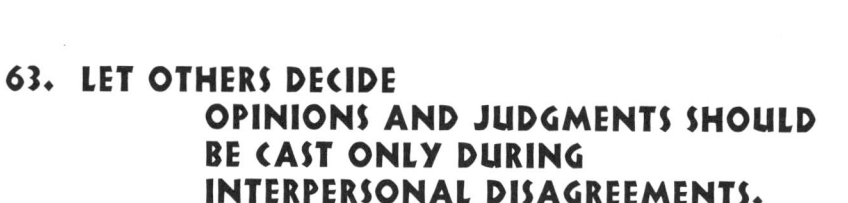

63. LET OTHERS DECIDE
   OPINIONS AND JUDGMENTS SHOULD BE CAST ONLY DURING INTERPERSONAL DISAGREEMENTS.

64. QUALITY IS A TRANSITORY MEASURE
   WHAT'S GOOD TODAY IS LANDFILL TOMORROW.

65. NEGATE NEGOTIATIONS DEMAND IT ALL.

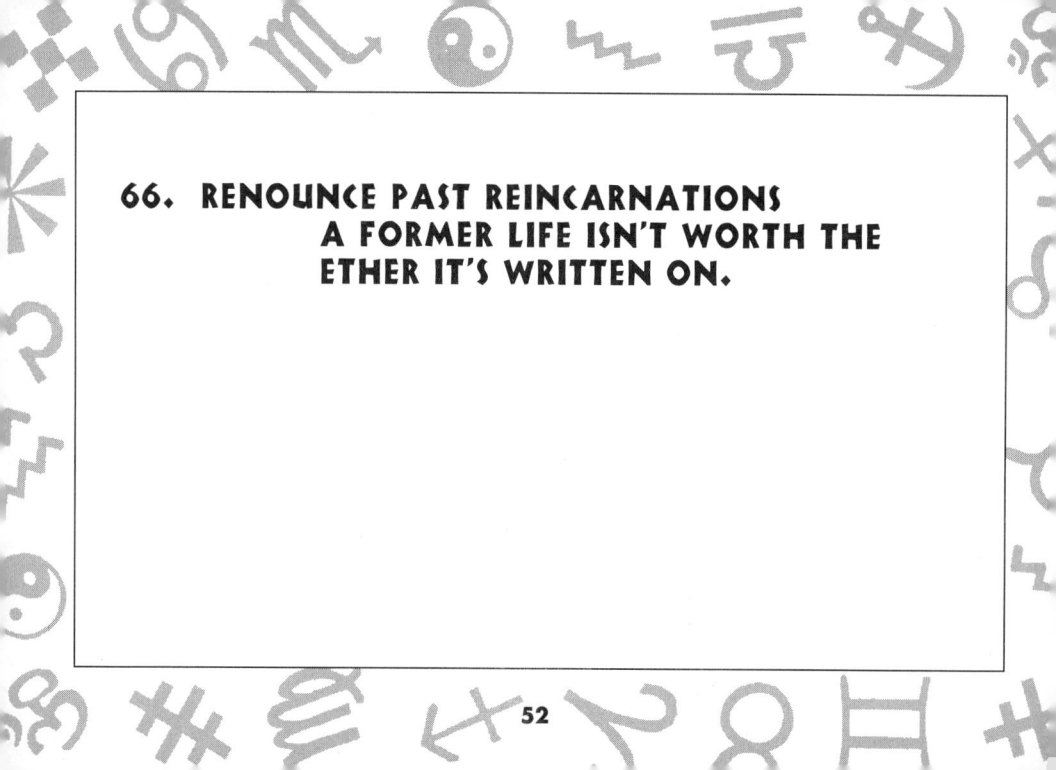

66. RENOUNCE PAST REINCARNATIONS
A FORMER LIFE ISN'T WORTH THE ETHER IT'S WRITTEN ON.

67. FIND SOLACE IN EXTRAVAGANT WASTE
   DON'T WORRY, THE WORLD'S
   RESOURCES WON'T RUN OUT UNTIL
   WELL AFTER YOUR DEATH.

68. SEND PHOTOCOPIES TO NO ONE
   A NON-EXISTENT PAPER TRAIL
   NEVER LEADS HOME.

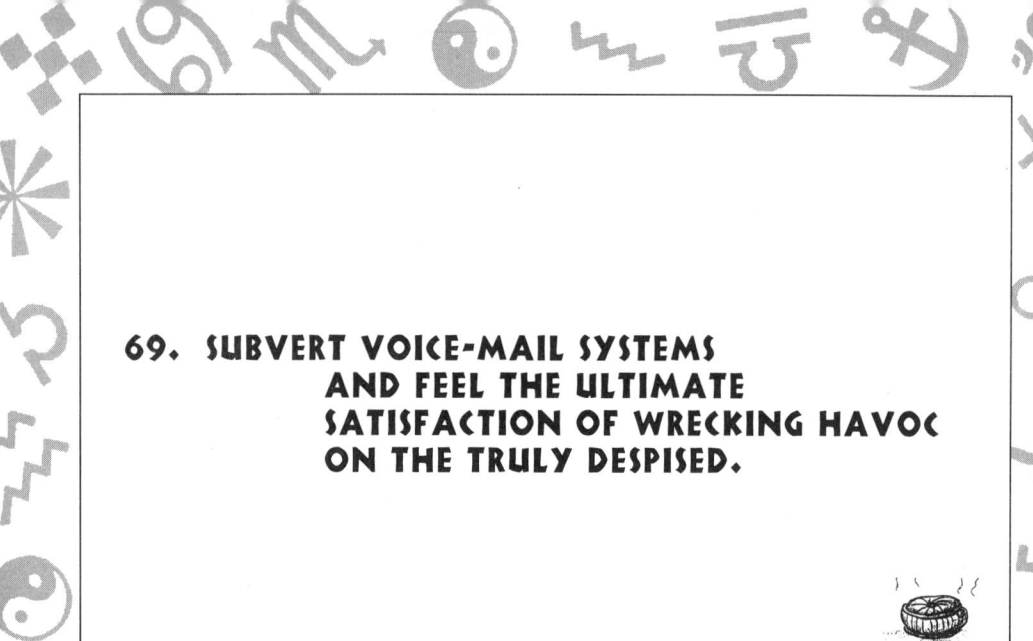

69. SUBVERT VOICE-MAIL SYSTEMS AND FEEL THE ULTIMATE SATISFACTION OF WRECKING HAVOC ON THE TRULY DESPISED.

**70. CHAMPION EXPECTATION
YOU'LL UNDOUBTEDLY BE
DISAPPOINTED ANYWAY.**

**71. FAVOR THE AUDACIOUS
EXTRAVAGANCE HAS NO FEAR.**

72. **DISAVOW THE RECEPTION OF INNOVATIVE IDEAS**

> YOU CAN ALWAYS CLAIM OWNERSHIP FOR THE SUCCESSFUL ONES AFTER THE FACT AND DISTRIBUTE BLAME FOR THOSE THAT AREN'T.

73. **IMPOSE PRETENTIOUSNESS LIBERALLY**

> CONSPICUOUS OSTENTATION IS SYMBOLIC OF A SUPERIOR AND FACILE INTELLIGENCE.

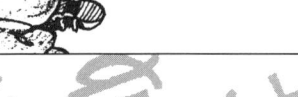

**74. ESPOUSE POLITICAL SENTIMENTS
      DEMOCRATS AND REPUBLICANS ARE
      LIFEMASTERS OF DESCENDENTALISM.**

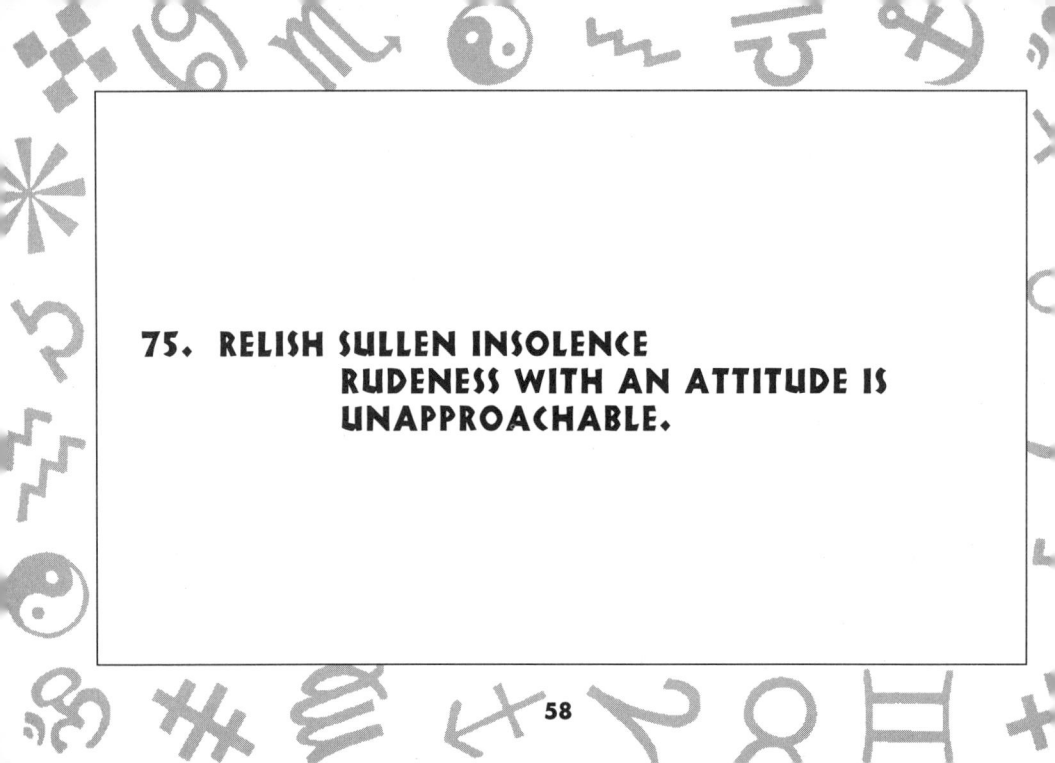

**75. RELISH SULLEN INSOLENCE
RUDENESS WITH AN ATTITUDE IS
UNAPPROACHABLE.**

76. **PLAGIARIZE WHENEVER POSSIBLE**
    DO NOT FORGET WHY GOD GAVE
    YOU EYES.

77. **EMBRACE BRAZEN SELF-CONTRADICTIONS**
    CONSISTENCY ONLY LEADS TO
    GREATER RESPONSIBILITY.

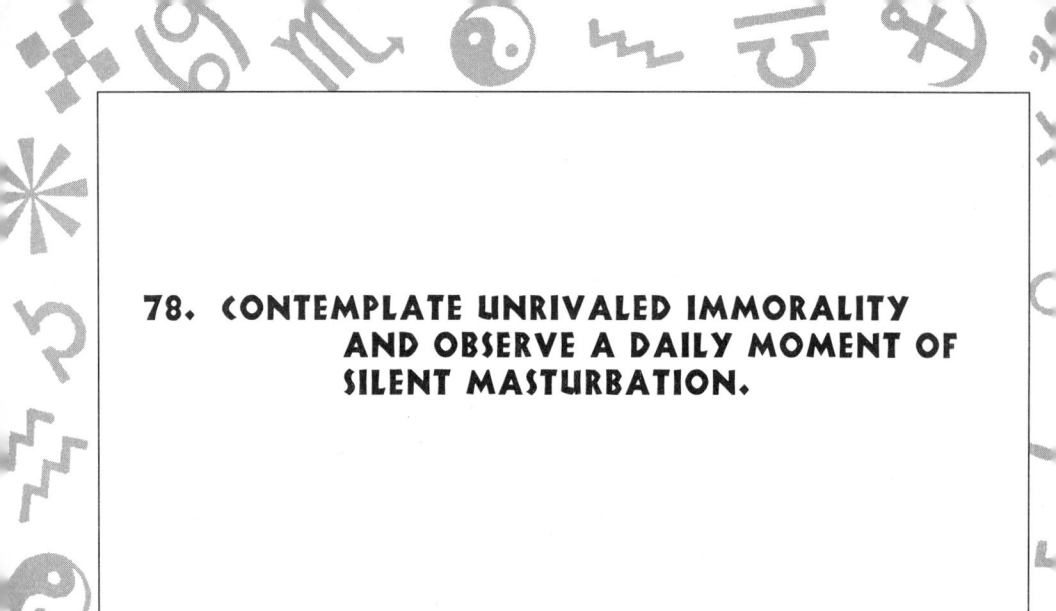

78. CONTEMPLATE UNRIVALED IMMORALITY AND OBSERVE A DAILY MOMENT OF SILENT MASTURBATION.

79. IGNORE PREVENTATIVE MAINTENANCE
    BREAKDOWNS ARE THE FALLOW
    TIMES OF THE SOUL.

80. DIVEST YOURSELF OF INVESTMENTS
    RISK AVERSION IS ITS OWN REWARD.

81. HOARD VAST INCOME
   MONEY IS NEVER OUT OF FASHION.

82. SHRED ACCOUNTS PAYABLE
   WHO'S TO SAY WHAT'S REALLY DUE AND WHEN?

83. DISPUTE GENETICS
EVERY CODE CAN BE BROKEN.

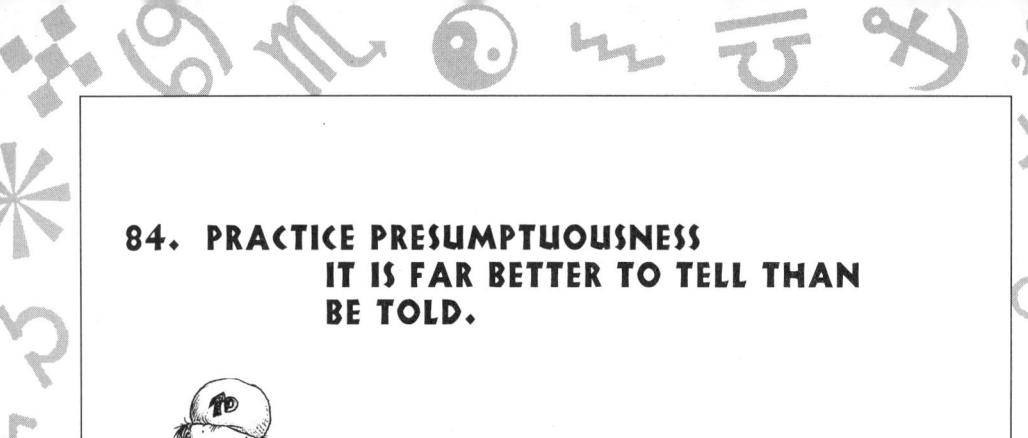

84. PRACTICE PRESUMPTUOUSNESS
IT IS FAR BETTER TO TELL THAN BE TOLD.

85. RELINQUISH LINEAL HEREDITY DENOUNCE GENERATIONAL EVOLUTION.

86. AVOID PERSONAL INTIMACY
    NEVER FALL PREY TO ANOTHER'S
    CHAIN OF DESIRE.

87. PRAISE DYSFUNCTIONAL FAMILIES
    THE FERTILIZER FOR A LIFE OF
    TOTAL DENIAL.

88. EXALT IN SUMPTUOUS MATERIALISM THE HAVES HAVE IT.

89. VISUALIZE SKEPTICISM
DEBUNK THE UNSEEN.

90. REVEL IN EXORBITANT SOIRÉES
   PARTY BEYOND TOLERANCE
   THERE ARE NO TIME LIMITS ON
   AVOIDANCE.

91. FOSTER SUPERFICIAL RELATIONSHIPS
   THEN EVEN WHEN YOU KNOW
   YOU'RE WRONG YOU CAN INSIST
   YOU'RE RIGHT.

**92. DISREGARD PRESCRIBED DIETING
DAMN THE SCALES,
FULL FAT AHEAD.**

**93. NEGLECT ATHLETIC EXERCISE
PHYSICAL FITNESS ONLY REDUCES
IQ POINTS.**

94. PROMOTE DESCENDENTAL MEDITATION UNCONSCIOUSNESS THROUGH DISTRACTION EQUALS HAPPINESS.

95. **ABSTAIN FROM LEADERSHIP**
    BETTER TO BLEAT THAN BLEED.

96. **GLORY IN GOSSIP**
    INQUIRING MINDS WILL TELL YOU
    WHETHER THEY KNOW OR NOT.

**97. BELIEVE IN SELF-DECEPTION
IF YOU CAN'T CONVINCE YOURSELF,
WHO CAN YOU CONVINCE?**

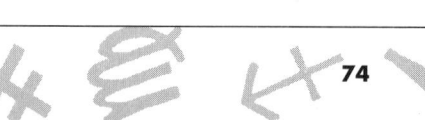

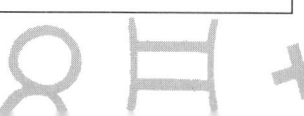

98. EMBRACE UNRESTRAINED GLUTTONY EATING HAS NEVER HAD ANYTHING TO DO WITH HUNGER.

**99. EXERCISE YOUR SUPERIORITY
     INFERIORS ARE ALWAYS HAPPIEST
     WHEN THEY KNOW THEIR PLACE.**

**100. MANIFEST SUPERSTITIOUS JUSTIFICATIONS
      AND DO THAT VOODOO
      YOU DO SO WELL.**

101. MISREPRESENT MIRACLES
   **THERE'S A SUCKER BORN
   EVERY MINUTE.**

102. RENOUNCE ANGELS
   **ALWAYS DEMAND CREDENTIALS
   FROM UNSOLICITED SALES.**

103. PURCHASE ENLIGHTENMENT
IF A MILLION BUCKS CAN'T BUY IT,
IT AIN'T WORTH IT.

104. SUPPORT UNRESTRICTED CONSUMPTIVE DEPENDENCIES
       GATHER SPIRITS WHERE YOU MAY.

105. LUXURIATE IN EXCESS
       SOMEONE HAS TO DO IT.

106. CLEAVE TO FANATICISM
    THOSE WHO STAND IN YOUR WAY
    ONLY THINK THEY KNOW.

107. RELEASE ZIPPERS
    ABSTINENCE GETS YOU NOWHERE.

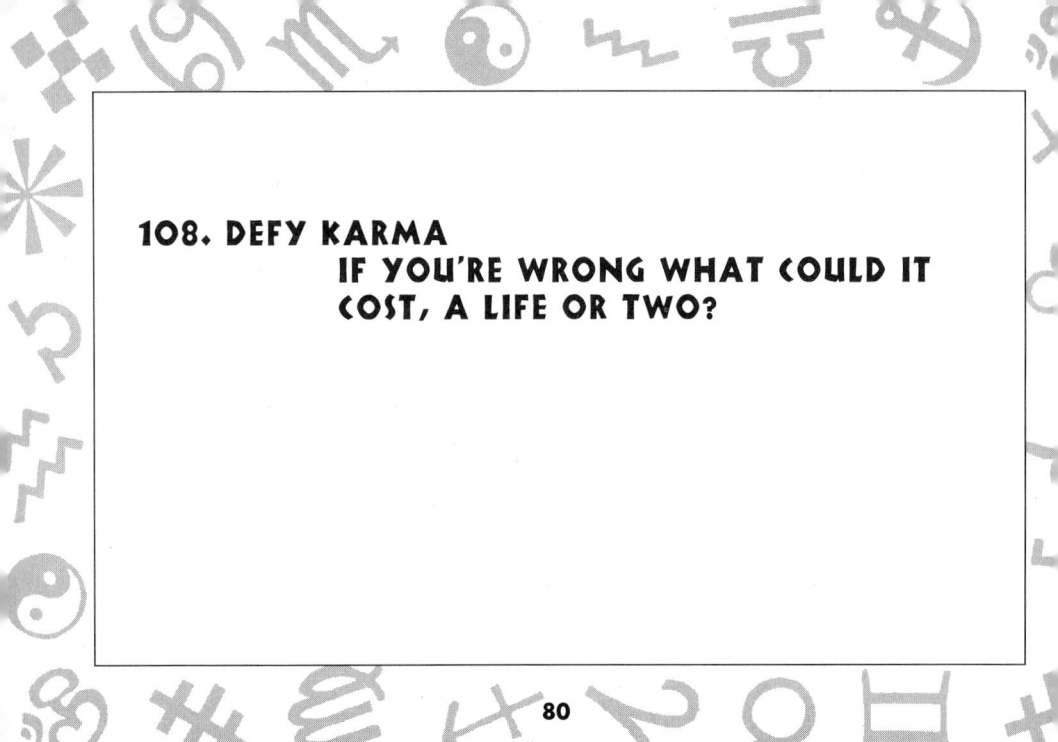

108. DEFY KARMA
IF YOU'RE WRONG WHAT COULD IT COST, A LIFE OR TWO?